WHEN LIFE GETS TOUGH

FINDING PEACE *and* STRENGTH
in TIMES *of* TROUBLE

Henry Gariepy

Honor Books is an imprint of
Cook Communications Ministries, Colorado Springs,
Colorado 80918
Cook Communications, Paris, Ontario
Kingsway Communications, Eastbourne, England

WHEN LIFE GETS TOUGH, FINDING PEACE AND
STRENGTH IN TIMES OF TROUBLE
© 2003 by Henry Gariepy

All rights reserved. No part of this book may be repro-
duced without written permission,
except for brief quotations in books and critical reviews.
For information, write Cook Communications Ministries,
4050 Lee Vance View, Colorado Springs, Colorado 80918.

First Printing, 2003
Printed in the United States of America

1 2 3 4 5 6 7 8 9 10 Printing/Year 07 06 05 04 03

Editor: W. Terry Whalin
Cover Design and Interior Design:
Greg Jackson, Jackson Design Co.

Unless otherwise noted, Scripture quotations are taken
from the Holy Bible: New International Version®
Copyright © 1973, 1978, 1984 by International Bible
Society. Used by permission of Zondervan Publishing
House. All rights reserved.

Library of Congress Cataloging-in-Publication Data
Applied For

Gariepy, Henry
When Life Gets Tough, Finding Peace and Strength in
Times of Trouble

p. cm.
ISBN 1-56292-501-6

CONTENTS

PREFACE

Crises may bring us to a personal point of "Ground Zero," where life seems shattered and its foundations are tested to the limit. As acknowledged in these pages, everyone will face trouble. Life often does get tough. For such times, the promises of the Bible provide an unfailing resource of sustaining grace. Each of the thoughts in this book is based on the Word of God.

Amid the storms of life, the Bible is our anchor that holds us steadfast; it is our compass that will chart the unknown way before us. As we make our way upon paths that may have been redefined by trouble, let us affirm with the psalmist of old, "Your word is a lamp to my feet and a light for my path" (Ps. 119:105).

For every reader, we pray that these insights from God's Word may bring comfort, guidance, and blessing. In particular, as this book makes its way to thousands of those involved in the September 11, 2001, tragedy, we pay tribute to the many brave and tireless workers and to the faith and courage of families who lost loved ones—or themselves suffered affliction—from these staggering catastrophes. Our Salvation Army workers and canteens were at the World Trade Center before the second plane struck and continued serving those at Ground Zero and families of the victims there as well as at the Pentagon, Western Pennsylvania, and related sites throughout the long days and nights and months following.

Some readers may want to use the content of this book as a daily reading, because the 31 chapters comprise a month of readings and are followed with a strategy for continuing on with life.

A sign in an old-fashioned tinker shop read, "We can mend anything except a broken heart." But an announcement has been posted in the Bible that says of our Heavenly Father, "He heals the brokenhearted and binds up their wounds" (Ps. 147:3). May these devotions be used of the Lord to bring healing and wholeness once again.

God hath not promised skies always blue,
Flower-strewn pathways all our lives through;
God hath not promised sun without rain,
Joy without sorrow, peace without pain.

God hath not promised we shall not know
Toil and temptation, trouble and woe;
He hath not told us we shall not bear
Many a burden, many a care.

But God hath promised strength for the day,
Rest for the labor, light for the way,
Grace for the trials, help from above,
Unfailing sympathy, undying love

~ANNIE JOHNSON FLINT

God cares and is there
to help and heal when life
comes tumbling down.

WHEN LIFE COMES TUMBLING DOWN

*God is our refuge and strength, an
ever-present help in trouble.* (Ps. 46:1)

Trouble eventually knocks at everyone's door.
Sometimes it doesn't bother to knock, it bangs
the door down—ruthlessly, violently, unexpected
and unwanted.

Job's plaintive warning echoes across the
centuries: "Man is born to trouble ... ." Sometimes
it is as a far off shadow, but inexorably it moves
closer and will surely come to our door.

So what do we do when trouble comes, when
life comes tumbling down about us? Do we seek to
run from it? Refuse to face reality? Give up?

Any glib and simple answers about trouble and
tragedy just do not ring true in a world where head-
lines scream to us of the millions of starving, the
plight of refugees, the inhumanity of the holocaust, the slaughters by terrorists, and the nuclear
nightmare that haunts every new generation.

"Bad things do not happen for any good reason," states Rabbi Harold Kushner in his book, *When Bad Things Happen to Good People*. "But," he tells us, "we can redeem these tragedies from senselessness by imposing meaning on them. The question we should be asking is not, 'Why did this happen to me?' That is really unanswerable. A better question would be, 'Now that this has happened to me, what am I going to do about it?'"

The psalmist invites us to put our trust in God as our refuge and strength. The God who cares is there to help and to heal when life comes tumbling down around us.

TODAY GOD IS REACHING OUT TO YOU.
WILL YOU REACH OUT TO HIM?

When shattering
experiences come,
God gives courage
and comfort.

THE ANTIDOTE TO FEAR

Therefore we will not fear. (Ps. 46:2)

When the forecast calls for a storm, ships need a sure anchor; trees, deep roots; persons, a firm foundation of faith.

Faith in God becomes the antidote to fear. Like the psalmist, we, too, can declare in the middle of life's crises, "Therefore we will not fear." Throughout the Bible there are 365 "fear nots" or its equivalent. God has given us one for every day of the year!

A symbol of arrogance is found in the epigram carved over a doorway on the Titanic: "Not even God can sink this ship." Its blasphemy still rots at the bottom of the Atlantic. Modern man is infected with the myth of self-sufficiency, of autonomy. The psalmist reminds us that we are insufficient in our own strength alone, that we need God as our refuge and strength for the trials and testings that surely will come our way.

This 46th Psalm became a major source of

12

comfort and courage in the aftermath of the terrorist attacks on America on September 11, 2001. The psalm was read on televised programs across the country. As described in the psalm, those things that had once seemed so secure came tumbling down upon us. Life could never again be the same. More than ever we have needed the assuring word that God is an ever-present help in trouble, and because He is with us, we need not fear.

Sooner or later stressful situations will beset each life, some striking us as emotional earth-quakes.

When shattering experiences come into your life, in place of fear God will give you courage and comfort.

At the helm
of the universe
God is in control.

GOD AT THE HELM

*You hem me in—behind and before; you have
laid your hand upon me. Such knowledge
is too wonderful for me ...* (Ps. 139:5–6)

If God is good and all-powerful, how can evil
exist? Why should God have visited untold
miseries upon the biblical character Job, His most
exemplary and faithful servant? Why does He allow
the death of innocent children, the violent attacks
on good people, the indiscriminate ravages of
famine, natural disaster, disease, and terrorism?
Why is there this individual and collective suffering?

How can God be absolved from such an
unfathomable mystery and meaningless fate? The
problem of the goodness of God in the middle of
evil and suffering can be accepted only in the light
of God's sovereignty. This big picture of God
provides the eternal rather than the temporal
perspective on our human condition.

The sovereignty of God is the one impreg-
nable rock to which the suffering human heart

14

must cling. The Scriptures assert God's supremacy over the evil that man's sin has brought into human existence. At the helm of the universe our sovereign God is in control. A faith in the sovereignty of God and His power to transform suffering into eternal good is the Christian's great weapon in his confronting life's inequities and calamities.

God does not "send" our suffering—it is the consequence of sin and Satan at work in the world. We live in a fallen world, and suffering is the common heritage of fallen humanity. But we can face life's evil knowing that it cannot thwart God's purposes for His children. The ultimate triumph is God's, and ours in Him.

TAKE A MOMENT AND ACKNOWLEDGE THAT GOD ULTIMATELY CONTROLS YOUR SITUATION. ASK GOD TO TAKE THE HELM OF YOUR LIFE.

When all is darkness,
faith gives the victory.

THE DARK NIGHT OF THE SOUL

My God, my God, why have you forsaken me? (Ps. 22:1)

Jesus spoke the words of this Psalm as His fourth saying from the cross. The Son of God uttered the words in that moment of experiencing the forsakenness of God as a consequence of bearing the world's sin.

Sooner or later, we, too, may feel like God has forsaken us. Saint John of the Cross named this experience "the dark night of the soul." In such times it seems that our prayers are but empty words, that God is hidden from us, and we bear our burden in a lonely universe.

During World War II, a nameless Jew hiding in Germany scratched on a basement wall the Star of David and the following lines: "I believe in the sun even when it is not shining. I believe in love even when I do not feel it. I believe in God even when He is silent."

In our Lord's dark night of the soul, He still

laid hold on God: "My God, my God." That affirmation will sustain us in our own dark night of the soul. In our greatest crisis, we can still have faith that God will ultimately work out His eternal purpose in our lives.

Faith gives the victory, when all is darkness, to still know the assurance of God's love and presence. When circumstances eclipse the sun from our sky, may we be able to still say, "My God, my God."

With the poet, Whittier, we affirm:

> *I know not where his islands lift*
> *Their fronded palms in air;*
> *I only know I cannot drift*
> *Beyond his love and care.*

WHEN YOU FEEL FORSAKEN, CRY OUT,
"MY GOD, MY GOD" AS AN AFFIRMATION
OF FAITH—EVEN IN THE SILENCE.

Life's true meaning lies close to the crosses of life.

LIFE'S UNEXPECTED CROSSES

*As they led him away, they seized Simon
from Cyrene ... and put the cross on him and
made him carry it behind Jesus. (Luke 23:26)*

As Christ was forced to carry His cross on the
Via Dolorosa, the "Road of Sorrows", His
strength had been sapped by the brutal scourging
and the travesty of trials through the night hours.
Proceeding with faltering steps, He sank beneath
the weight of the cross. Soldiers, impatient with
this delay, grab hold of an onlooker, Simon, and
press him into service.

It must have been an extreme annoyance, an
indignity, and a heavy load to carry up a steep hill.
Simon's own business had to be put on hold, and
touching that instrument of death felt revolting.
He did not deserve it. He could not tell why; he
simply knew he was compelled to bear an unexpected cross.

Simon of Cyrene is typical of all human life.

He is only one of an innumerable company who have been compelled to bear heavy and unexpected crosses. Life is full of Simons and unexpected crosses.

For some of us, only yesterday life flowed along like a song. No clouds were in sight. Then, suddenly, a storm burst upon us in all its fury. With it came an unexpected cross we were compelled to carry.

Life's true meaning lies close to the crosses of life and to the cross Jesus carried that day. Scripture reveals that Simon and his family found a living faith as a result of his carrying that cross.

WHEN LIFE THRUSTS AN UNEXPECTED CROSS ON YOUR LIFE, DEDICATE YOUR CROSS TO THE ONE WHO WAS THE ULTIMATE CROSS BEARER FOR THE WORLD.

The Lord's presence sustains us, and His promise stretches past the darkness into the brightness of day.

ABIDE WITH ME

Stay with us, for it is nearly evening;
the day is almost over. (Luke 24:29)

In one of the most beautiful accounts in the New
Testament, following His resurrection, Jesus
appeared to two of his followers on the road to
Emmaus. For them, it was a road of disappointment, of heartbreak, of defeat. Their bright
dreams of tomorrow had been turned into the
grim nightmare of Calvary.

They did not recognize Christ, and as they
approached their destination He seemed ready to
take leave of them and go on. But following His
luminous discourse with them, they urged Him to
stay with them as evening was falling.

To each life there comes the time when the
shadows of evening fall upon our pathway, and we
need the presence of the Lord. It is evening for our
world when hope seems hard to find. It is evening
for our families when troubles come. It is evening
for us when we experience loss, illness, grief, or

tragedy. And nightfall often comes with death.

When the evening times of life come, we would ask the risen Lord, as did the disciples of old, "Abide with us." His presence sustains us and His promise stretches past the darkness into the brightness of day. As those two companions of old, we, too, will rejoice in the glow of His presence as He turns our Good Friday into Easter Sunday.

> *Abide with me, fast falls the eventide.*
> *The darkness deepens; Lord, with me abide.*
> *When other helpers fail and comforts flee,*
> *Help of the helpless, oh, abide with me.*

TAKE A MOMENT TO STAND AND
READ ALOUD THIS PRAYER.

Misfortune never leaves us where it finds us.

LIFE IS NOT FAIR

What I dreaded has happened to me. (Job 3:25)

Relentless pain racked Job's body, his memory tortured him with the loss of his children. In that moment, his wife suggested he curse God and kill himself.

Job's pent up torment erupted, and from the depths of his anguish he cried out against his suffering. No fewer than 14 times his anger exploded with a curse; 14 times he hurled his anger at the heavens.

However, his curses and protests were not against God but against his own contemptible circumstances. Job wished he had never been born, that his birthday could be erased from the calendar. But having been born, he now wished that death would release him from his suffering. His poignant cry described a man who had hit bottom and had nothing to live for: "What I feared has come upon me; what I dreaded has happened to me." Job had reached his Ground Zero.

In his best-selling book Rabbi Kushner reminds us: "Life is not fair. The wrong people get sick and the wrong people get robbed and the wrong people get killed in wars and in accidents." Job is the classic example of bad things happening to good people.

Suffering is an inevitable part of life. Misfortune never leaves us where it finds us. The pain will one day cease. But what we learn in these dark experiences is our treasure forever.

As Job of old, we may find that life is not fair, and what we dreaded has come into our life. But our testing and trial can lead us into a closer walk with God. And our turning to God shines His light in the dark place of our soul and brightens our path.

IN THE MIDDLE OF YOUR TRIAL OR SUFFERING WHEN YOUR LIFE IS NOT FAIR, TURN TO GOD AND ASK FOR HIS PEACE AND COMFORT.

When the outlook
is not good,
let us take the uplook.

A PRAYER-ANSWERING GOD

You will pray to him, and he will hear you. (Job 22:27)

Job's friend uttered a fundamental truth in this counsel to Job, who needed the sustaining strength that comes only through prayer.

We need the power of prayer for our daily living, tasks, and struggles. Nothing lies outside the reach of prayer except a prayer outside the will of God.

Our modern life is consumed with a tornado of activity, a torrent of voices, a tumult of noise. Each day we need a sanctuary of solitude where we may replenish our spent resources, a place of quiet where we can hear the soft accents of the Eternal. Prayer is pivotal for our lives. We will be better or worse, strong or weak, as we pray more or less. In prayer, our weakness is linked to the Almighty, our ignorance to God's wisdom, and our finite lives to the infinite God. "He who has learned to pray," declared William Law, "has learned the secret of a holy and happy life."

Only as we near the end of the Book of Job—where he enters into communion with God—does Job emerge triumphant in his trial. When he stops talking and starts listening to God, a dramatic transformation takes place. As a child of God, we too have this remarkable resource and experience.

Prayer is the nearest approach to God, the noblest exercise of the soul, and our greatest source of power. When trouble comes, we must work as though everything depends on us and pray as though everything depends on God.

WHEN YOUR OUTLOOK IS NOT GOOD, TRY TURNING TO A PRAYER-ANSWERING GOD. PRAYER WILL MAKE ALL THE DIFFERENCE IN YOUR SITUATION.

The Bible provides
our needed
survival strategies.

THE CRISIS OF CHANGE

Jesus Christ is the same yesterday
and today and forever. (Heb. 13:8)

Many of us can remember when "setting the world on fire" was merely a figure of speech, only preachers were preparing people to travel to outer space, a floppy disk was something you consulted your chiropractor about, and people were smarter than machines. Dynamic change is a trademark of our times. As Bob Dylan sang, "The times, they are a changin'!"

It has often been said since September 11, 2001, that life will never be the same again. In a matter of minutes, our nation was changed from a country of peaceful security to a place vulnerable to the monstrous acts of terrorism and threatened with weapons of mass destruction.

The crisis of change also occurs on a personal level. Today we may march forth in health and vigor. Suddenly, sickness unhinges our knees and we become horizontal citizens of the sickroom,

26

unwilling initiates into the fellowship of pain. Misfortune can overtake us in a moment, shatter our dreams, and bring us to the brink of desperation.

Alvin Toffler's popular book, *Future Shock,* was written to "help us survive our collision course with tomorrow" as we face "the death of permanence." It was designed as a textbook with strategies for survival for those overwhelmed by change and its impacts.

But, of course, we already have a textbook for coping with the crisis of change. The Bible provides the needed survival strategies and tells us of the One who remains unchanging in our changing world.

IN THE SWIRL OF CHANGE, COMMIT TO CLING TO THE ONE WHO NEVER CHANGES FOR YOUR STRENGTH.

We can never calculate
the debt the world
owes to sorrow.

IN THE SCHOOL
OF SORROW

Then the LORD answered Job
out of the storm. (Job 38:1)

Biblical and secular history is replete with examples of God speaking to His children in the storms of life. Not only has He spoken to them, but also He has spoken through them. We can never calculate the debt the world owes to sorrow.

Most of the psalms and messages of the prophets have come to us out of the crucible of suffering and trial. The New Testament epistles were written mostly in prison. The greatest poets often "learned in suffering what they taught in song."

When things go well it is possible to live for years on the surface of things. But when sorrow comes, a man is driven to the deep things of life and God. Sorrow becomes the expositor of mysteries that joy leaves unexplained.

Many share the sentiment of an unknown poet:

28

I walked a mile with Pleasure,
She chatted all the way,
But left me none the wiser
For all she had to say.
I walked a mile with Sorrow,
And ne'er a word said she,
But, oh the things I learned from her
When Sorrow walked with me!

When we walk along the shore of the ocean, we note that the rocks are sharp in the quiet coves but polished in those places where the waves beat against them. If we allow Him, God can use the "waves" of life that beat against us to polish and beautify our souls.

How is God using your waves
of life to polish your soul?

When crisis strikes, we need to find some quiet moments, to hear the still, small voice of God.

THE POWER OF SILENCE

Be still, and know that I am God. (Ps. 46:10)

The psalmist, in time of trouble, calls us to the recreating stillness of the soul. To "be still" is often opposite of what we tend to do when stress hits our life.

A mighty power resides in silence. Gravity, a silent force, holds stars and galaxies in their orbits. Sunbeams make their long journey to earth without any sound, yet they bear an immense energy. The dew falls silently, yet brings refreshment and beauty. Nature's mighty miracles are wrought in silence. The wheels of the universe do not creak. Noise and confusion come from man.

It's so easy to lose our way amid our sound-soaked days and nights. When a crisis strikes, we need to find some quiet moments, an interval away from the confusion and noise about us. Then we can hear the still, small voice of God calling us to restoration and wholeness.

In the heart of Crawford Notch in the White

Mountains of New Hampshire, the waters of the Saco River form a small pool. The mountain winds are usually rushing down through the Notch and ruffling the surface with a continual disturbance. But at times the winds are hushed and the waters still, and then its mirrored surface catches and reflects perfectly the towering cliffs of Mount Webster and the infinite blue depths of the sky.

Only when the winds and storms of the world that blow across our lives are quieted can we catch and reflect the beauty of the Infinite. The psalmist invites us, "Be still, and know that I am God."

DECIDE TO SLIP AWAY FOR A FEW MINUTES FROM ANY NOISE. AS YOU SIT IN SILENCE, FILL YOUR MIND WITH GOD.

God comes to us
through the love, prayer,
and caring of others.

WHERE IS GOD?

When you pass through the waters,
I will be with you. (Isa. 43:2)

Elie Wiesel has quickened the conscience of our generation with his book, *Night,* which relates his experience in the holocaust. A teenage Jew, he saw his fellow Jews herded into cattle cars and taken to the death camp. His mother, young sister, and all his family, disappeared into an oven fueled with human flesh. His memory seared with scenes of babies pitchforked, children hanged, and fellow prisoners living like animals, the question resonated around him, "Where is God?"

Indeed, where is God when innocent people suffer injustice and cruelty? Where is God when wrong is on the throne and right is on the gallows? Gordon MacDonald, well-known author and pastor, was led to serve with the Salvation Army's workers at Ground Zero of New York's World Trade Center in days following September 11. He recorded in his diary, "More than once I asked myself, as everyone asks, 'Is God here?' And I decided that He is closer to this place than any other place I've ever been. Amid this absolute catastrophe of unspeakable proportions, there is a beautiful spirit that defies the imagination. Everyone is everyone else's brother or sister at the work site. Tears ran freely, affection was exchanged openly, exhaustion was defied. Being on that street, giving cold water to workmen, praying and weeping with them, listening to their stories, was the closest I have ever felt to God."

Robert Browning cautions, "Hush, I pray you! What if this friend happens to be God?" God comes to us through the love, prayer, and caring of others.

TODAY MAKE A CONSCIOUS EFFORT TO REACH OUT
AND PRAY FOR A NEIGHBOR OR HELP A FRIEND
WITH SOMETHING—MAYBE A LISTENING EAR. YOU
CAN REPRESENT GOD TO OTHERS.

Trouble is the common lot of our humanity.

SONGS IN THE NIGHT

By day the LORD directs his love,
at night his song is with me. (Ps. 42:8)

Sooner or later, each of us reaches our night
season of life. Pain and suffering wear a thousand guises. Accident or disaster may shatter our
lives. An illness or death may rob us of a beloved,
or its dread shadow may hover over such a one.
We may be compelled to watch a loved one suffer
or see a promising young life wither or die.
Trouble is the common lot of our humanity.

A Hasidic saying states there are three ways in
which a man expresses sorrow. The man on the
lowest level cries; the man on the second level is
silent; the man on the highest level turns his
sorrow into song. The psalmist—and succeeding
generations of God's people—have found that
God turns our sorrows into songs.

The song in the night God has for us may be
the word or presence of a comforting friend. It
may come on the wings of an insight that will help

us to get through. In a thousand ways, God comes to His children in their night seasons with His presence and promise, as a song in the night. Fanny Crosby's hymns have inspired millions. She was incredibly prolific, composing over 6,000 hymns. She did her composing in a dark room, total darkness—she was blind. But God lit a light in her mind and soul that enabled her to see and share "rivers of pleasure" and "visions of rapture" that found their way into her songs. God gave her songs in the night that will resonate throughout time.

With the psalmist and the people of God, we, too, can find that "at night his song is with me."

TAKE YOUR FAVORITE SONG OR CHORUS
AND FOCUS ON THE WORDS THROUGHOUT TODAY
FOR YOUR STRENGTH AND COMFORT.

God turns our sorrows
into symphonies.

SORROWS INTO SYMPHONIES

God ... gives songs in the night. (Job 35:10)

In the classic musical, Phantom of the Opera, we hear the hauntingly beautiful melody and words: "I compose the music of the night. Close your eyes and let music set you free. Let your darker side give in to the power of the music that I write, the power of the music of the night." In a deeper and spiritual sense, this is the experience of God's people. God is the Composer of the music of the night, music that in our dark experiences affirms that we belong to Him who sets us free from the darkness.

Job in the Bible experienced the saddest woes of all as his whole world came tumbling down. In his despair, his friend came to him with the message: "God gives songs in the night."

When the black curtain of catastrophe fell on his soul, in his darkest hour a shaft of brilliant sunlight broke through Job's midnight sky. He gave the centuries a sublime song, which Handel incorporated in his immortal Messiah: "I know that my Redeemer lives!" (Job 19:25).

God turns our sorrows into symphonies. Job was but the forerunner of a great company to whom God has given songs in the night; songs born in the crucible of their adversity.

When our road becomes steeper, when our load becomes heavier, when our pain reaches deeper, when our night grows darker, in such a night season of the soul, let us listen, for surely we, too, will find with Job of old—and with countless others—that "God gives songs in the night."

Speak these words of faith, "I know my Redeemer lives," and "God gives me songs in the night."

God gives strength sufficient for today.

STRENGTH FOR TODAY

Your strength will equal your days. (Deut. 33:25)

God does not equip us with strength for tomorrow's troubles before they arrive. For each day He gives strength sufficient to see us through. As the old prayer affirms, "Lord help me to remember that nothing can happen to me today that You and I cannot handle together."

We may wonder how we could ever handle certain situations—the loss of a loved one, the onset of sickness, or an unimaginable tragedy. When we reach our personal "Ground Zero" and draw near to God, we find His presence and comfort become sufficient for today. We discover a new strength and upholding power. The poet has beautifully expressed this assuring truth:

He giveth more grace as our burdens grow greater,
He sendeth more strength as our labors increase,
To added afflictions, he addeth his mercy,
To multiplied trials he multiplies peace.

When we have exhausted our store of endurance,
When our strength has failed e're the day is half-done,
When we reach the end of our hoarded resources
Our Father's full giving is only begun.

His love has no limits, his grace has no measure,
His power no boundary known unto men;
For out of his infinite riches in Jesus
He giveth and giveth and giveth again.

ASK GOD TO GIVE YOU TODAY'S STRENGTH.

Earthly life is
but the preface
to our unending eternal
life with God.

THE ULTIMATE SAFETY

Do not be afraid of those who kill the body
but cannot kill the soul. (Matt. 10:28)

After the great Chicago fire of 1871, Mr.
Spafford, a Chicago lawyer, arranged an
ocean voyage to Europe for his family, where he
would join them later. The ship on which the
happy family sailed never got halfway across the
Atlantic. In the dead of night another ship rammed
their vessel and cut it in two. In the confusion and
disaster that followed, Mrs. Spafford saw all four
of her daughters swept away to their deaths. When
she and a few other survivors reached Wales, she
cabled two words to her husband: "Saved alone."

Taking the earliest available ship, he hurried
to see his wife, feeling all the ache of his heart
going out to her. When his ship reached the
approximate spot where the Ville du Havre had
met with disaster, God gave him the inspiration
and courage to write the words of the hymn that
has blessed countless:

When peace like a river attendeth my way,
When sorrows like sea-billows roll,
Whatever my lot, Thou has taught me to say:
It is well, it is well with my soul.

Jesus warned that the preservation of our soul is our ultimate security. The body is temporal yet the soul is eternal. Some people foresee the after-life of the soul as an appendix to a book of which life on earth constitutes the text. In reality, our earthly life is the preface to our unending eternal life with God.

Let us live so that whatever comes into our life, we will be able to claim for ourselves the assurance, "It is well, it is well with my soul."

YOUR ETERNAL ASSURANCE IS IN THE HANDS OF GOD.

In the eternal providence
of God will come
the springtime
of new life in Him.

THE ULTIMATE TRIUMPH

Weeping may remain for a night, but
rejoicing comes in the morning. (Ps. 30:5)

Theodore Roosevelt once returned home from a big game hunting trip in Africa. When he boarded the ship at the African port the red carpet was rolled out for him. Crowds gathered at the dock and applauded him. Roosevelt was given the finest suite on board, and all through the voyage he was the center of attention.

At the same time an old missionary who had given his life for his Lord in Africa boarded the ship. Now, his wife dead, children gone, himself old and worn out, he was returning home to America. No one noticed him, no one applauded a lonely old man.

When the ship docked at San Francisco, again Roosevelt was the focus of attention. Bells rang and whistles blew as he landed amid pomp and ceremony. But no one welcomed the old missionary.

Arriving at a small hotel, that night the missionary knelt and prayed, "Lord, I am not complaining. I gave my life for You in Africa, but it seems that no one cares. Lord, I don't understand."

Then it seemed that the Lord reached down from Heaven, laid His hand on the old man's shoulder, and said, "Missionary, you're not home yet!"

The poet Shelley lyricized: "If winter comes, can spring be far behind?" As winter storms beat across the landscape of our lives, so in the eternal providence of God will come the warmth and the springtime of new life in Him.

"No eye has seen, no ear has heard, no mind has conceived what God has prepared for those who love him" (1 Cor. 2:9).

YOU CAN BE CONFIDENT OF GOD'S
CONSTANT CARE FOR YOUR LIFE.

Trials, surrendered to God,
produce character and golden faith.

GOD KNOWS

But he knows the way that I take. (Job 23:10)

Job testified that though God may have seemed far away, God really knew him and his path of suffering. In one of the most affirming verses in this book, Job declared, "He knows the way that I take; when he has tested me, I will come forth as gold."

God knows. He knows the storms that buffet our lives. He knows the trials that we must endure. He knows the sorrows that afflict us. He knows the cross we are called to carry. He knows the rugged path we must travel. He knows, He understands, and He will be by our side to help and sustain.

It is an incredible thought, that the Creator and Governor of the mighty universe knows me and the way that I take. It is a comforting thought, that the One who holds the stars on their unerring courses holds my finite life in His mighty hands.

Job's faith was tested to its limits, right up to "Ground Zero." But he came through his furnace of affliction with a faith that was refined and purified.

44

As fire reveals the purity of gold, so affliction refines and reveals the purity of a life. In the end, Job's faith and trust, which already had made him a model in God's sight, enabled him to "come forth as gold."

God never wastes suffering. Trials, surrendered to the will of God, produce character and golden faith.

The words of a chorus echo the truth of our text:

He knows, He knows
The storms that would my way oppose;
He know, He knows
And tempers every wind that blows.

DESPITE YOUR LIFE'S STORMS, GOD KNOWS ABOUT AND CARRIES YOU THROUGH EVERY EXPERIENCE.

Heroes and heroines
are recorded
against a backdrop of
struggle and strife.

THE WOUNDED HEALER

He was pierced for our transgressions ...
and by his wounds we are healed. (Isa. 53:5)

The caliber and character of a person is found in an ability to meet disappointment or trial successfully. The chronicles of heroines and heroines are recorded against a backdrop of struggle and strife.

Joni Eareckson Tada, a quadriplegic from a diving accident, has been confined in a wheelchair for over 20 years. How does she view her handicap? She says: "My paralysis has drawn me close to God and given a spiritual healing which I wouldn't trade for a hundred active years on my feet. His grace enables me to rejoice, not in spite of my disability, but because of my disability."

At first she found her condition impossible to reconcile with her faith in a loving God. After three years of bitterness, tears, and violent questionings, one night her whole outlook was transformed. Pain was streaking through her back due

46

to her paralysis. One of her closest friends was beside her bed, searching desperately for some way to encourage her. Finally, she clumsily blurted out, "Joni, Jesus knows how you feel—He was paralyzed too."

Joni glared at her. "What? What are you talking about?" Her friend continued, "It's true. He was nailed on a cross, and He was paralyzed there."

It had never occurred to Joni that the Son of God had felt the same piercing pain that racked her body. "God became incredibly close to me," she says, "and I realized that God understands and loves me." Joni's ministry for the disabled has been a benediction to countless men and women around the globe.

JESUS KNOWS YOUR PAIN, AND THROUGH
THE CROSS YOU ARE HEALED.

When you face life's storms,
the foundations of life
will enable you to endure.

BUILDING THE FOUNDATION

I have no rest, but only turmoil. (Job 3:26)

The Book of Job in the Bible is every man's story. Each of us is engaged in a life-and-death struggle with the forces of evil. The drama of Job, who suffered the greatest calamities of anyone in the Bible, is a mirror reflecting our trials and struggles.

When you read Job, you will not find glib answers to the problem of suffering and evil in the world. The devout reader will find a perspective that enables him to see past the suffering and move from the "why" to the "who" that sustains us to conquer the trial.

Above all, the story of Job is one of triumph. In his trials, we see the grace of God that brings blessing from brokenness, celebration from calamity, and triumph from tragedy. In Job we encounter an unsurpassed moment of Old Testament faith when he stakes his destiny on the living Redeemer who "in the end ... will stand upon the earth" (19:25).

When trial or tragedy strikes, Job's story teaches that our foundation determines our response. When the storms of adversity beat on us, our bedrock faith as a foundation enables us to endure. It is not the gales which blow that determine the direction of a ship, but as the poet reminds us:

> *As we voyage along through life,*
> *'Tis the set of a soul*

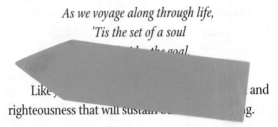

Like y̲ and righteousness that will sustain ̲ ̲g.

THROUGH YOUR TOUGH TIMES OF LIFE,
YOU CAN REST ON THE FOUNDATION OF GOD'S
ULTIMATE TRIUMPH FOR YOUR LIFE.

The Lord will guide us
through the dark
and difficult places.

A GOLDEN PROMISE

For the LORD God is a sun and shield. (Ps. 84:11)

T he psalmist, often writing in similes and
metaphors, says the Lord is to us as a sun. He
is our source of light, guidance, beauty, and life.
He will guide us through the dark and difficult
places.

To one who asked, "Give me a light that I may
tread safely into the unknown," came the reply:
"Go out into the darkness and put your hand into
the hand of God. That shall be to you better than a
light and safer than a known way."

The psalmist, using a metaphor of the defen-
sive weaponry of his day, says the Lord is our
shield. We are engaged in a life-and-death struggle. There is no demilitarized zone for the
Christian. No war is fought with greater fierceness
than the spiritual combat in our life. Foes are
present both without and within. We need a shield
to withstand the fierce assaults of Satan and to
triumph over the trials and testings of life. The

Lord as our Shield protects and enables us to be victorious.

The story is told of the famed Scot hero Robert Bruce who, when fleeing his enemies, took refuge in a cave and prayed for God's protection. While he was in the cave, a spider wove a web across its entrance. His pursuers came to the cave, but seeing the spider web across its opening thought Bruce could not have entered without breaking the web and went on their way. Later Bruce said, "Without God, a stone wall is as a spider web; with God a spider web is as a stone wall."

GOD IS YOUR LIGHT AND YOUR PROTECTION
FOR WHATEVER YOU FACE TODAY.

We do not stay
in death,
but walk through
its valley.

OUR GOOD SHEPHERD

The LORD is my Shepherd. (Ps. 23:1)

Psalm 23 has been one of the best-loved texts and brightest jewels of the Bible. Its timeless truths are as up-to-date as tomorrow's newscast. The psalmist doesn't refer to the Lord as "the" shepherd, but rather as "my" shepherd. He speaks with confidence about the Lord's knowledge of and personal care for him.

When our energies are spent and our spiritual resources seem exhausted, we need replenishment for our soul. "He restores my soul" is the assurance of the Lord's provision for our renewal. Our Good Shepherd will renew our inner resources, lift our spirits, and enable us to go on.

Death, called "the king of terror" holds no fear for the one who is in the Shepherd's care. With the psalmist we affirm, "Even though I walk through the valley of the shadow of death, I will fear no evil."

"Walk" indicates movement. Death is not the

end but a continued progress in the plan of God. We do not stay in death but walk through its valley. Death is but a passageway to the new, bright, shining world where our Good Shepherd leads us.

This radiant psalm reminds us that death is not substance but shadow. To create a shadow, there must be light. We look beyond the shadow of death to He who is "The Light of the World." The psalmist affirms, "I will fear no evil, for you are with me." Fear of death is eclipsed by the presence of our Good Shepherd, whose peerless gift is eternal life.

YOU CAN WALK THROUGH THE VALLEY OF THE
SHADOW OF DEATH HOLDING THE HAND
OF YOUR GOOD SHEPHERD.

God will make us
adequate
for life's testings.

53

MADE ADEQUATE

*My God will meet all your needs
according to his glorious riches
in Christ Jesus. (Phil. 4:19)*

While studying at Temple University in
Philadelphia, I would on occasion slip into
the basement chapel of the famed old Baptist
Temple on campus that flourished under the
powerful preaching of Russell Conwell. It is called
the Chapel of the Four Chaplains and memorial-
izes with a graphic mural one of the great acts of
heroism in World War II.

Clark Poling was a preacher, son of one of
America's most distinguished clergymen and
father of a lovely family. He was called to serve as a
chaplain during World War II. During those dark
days, he wrote to his family and parents: "I know I
shall have your prayers, but please don't pray
simply that God will keep me safe. War is danger-
ous business. Pray that God will make me
adequate."

The troop ship Dorchester, on which he was serving, was torpedoed off the west coast of Iceland. As the ship was going down, Clark Poling and the three other chaplains on board handed their life jackets to four servicemen. They were last seen on the slanting deck of the ship. With linked arms and hearts in prayer, somewhere in the icy Atlantic, four men were cheating death because of their sacrifice. That act of heroism became a national symbol of interfaith sacrifice. In that moment, the prayers for Clark Poling were abundantly answered. God made him adequate.

God will not always protect us from danger, but when we are living for Him and call upon Him, He will make us adequate for life's testings and trials.

GOD WILL BE ADEQUATE FOR EVERY
SITUATION IN YOUR LIFE.

God's power
is made perfect
in our weakness.

THE PARADOX OF POWER

For when I am weak, then I am strong. (2 Cor. 12:10)

Life is full of paradoxes, or statements, which seem self-contradictory yet in fact may be true. Subtle truths are often clothed in paradoxes in the Bible, such as "Believing is seeing," and "Whoever saves his life loses his life." These statements are puzzles asking to be solved or mysteries craving to be unraveled.

The apostle Paul gives us the paradox, "For when I am weak, then I am strong." This statement especially seems strange in our power-conscious, power-driven age that projects the macho image and boasts of megatons and megabytes. Modern man worships at the shrine of power. But the Apostle actually says that he delights in his weakness. Why?

Paul discovered the great secret that as his self-sufficiency surrendered to God's great sufficiency, God takes our weakness and changes it into strength. The Lord Himself told the Apostle, "My grace is sufficient for you, for my power is made perfect in weakness" (2 Cor. 12:9).

Submission is strength. It is not weakness for the boat with a sail to submit to the laws of aerodynamics. The law enables the boat to harness the wind's strength and use it to give power and direction. When we submit to the Lord of the universe, our finiteness is lost in His mighty power, realizing our highest potential and enabling us to go forward.

If we have been trying to cope in our own strength with the challenges of life, let us discover the Lord's grace will be sufficient for our need and believe God's power is made perfect in weakness.

IF YOU ARE FEELING WEAK, GOD'S GRACE
WILL BE SUFFICIENT BECAUSE HIS POWER
IS MADE PERFECT IN WEAKNESS.

Whatever
the future holds,
I'm in His hands.

FAITH IN THE STORM

Then [Job] fell to the ground in worship. (Job 1:20)

A hurricane of woes had thundered on Job with all its fury. Without intermission, he heard the recital of worsened catastrophes.

Job may well have turned to his wife and said, "We've lost all our possessions, but at least we still have that which is most precious—our children." Just then, a messenger came with the worst news of all: "Your children are all dead, killed when a whirlwind collapsed their house." Such words strike as a sharp arrow in the tender heart of an unsuspecting parent. In one shattering moment, ten vibrant, beautiful lives ceased to be. And the richest man in the East was suddenly, in successive strokes of calamity, stripped of possessions and family. Job lost everything.

In this moment, Job fell to the ground, not in despair or defeat; but rather we read, "in worship." Job survived the storm. His faith stood firm.

58

When great testing or trial comes upon us, in the words of Stanley Ditmer's hymn, we affirm:

I shall not fear
though darkened clouds may gather round me;
The God I serve is one who cares and understands.
Although the storms I face
would threaten to confound me,
Of this I am assured: I'm in his hands.
I'm in his hands, I'm in his hands;
What e'er the future holds, I'm in his hands,
The days I cannot see, have all been planned for me;
His way is best, you see; I'm in his hands.

DESPITE THE STORMS OF LIFE,
YOU CAN REST IN GOD'S HANDS.

Christ's resurrection
solved the riddle of death.

LIFE AFTER DEATH

If a man dies, will he live again? (Job 14:14)

Job asked the universal question. He put into words the yearning of all humanity.

This ancient question echoes across the centuries and remains the central question of life. Inscriptions on tombs of tribes extinct for centuries offer mute testimony to man's ancient quest for immortality.

Posed as an anxious question, Job referred to death as "the king of terrors" and "a journey of no return." Death imposes for many a certain fear and anxiety. The question exposes Job's hope and quest for immortality.

The schools of philosophy cannot answer Job's question. It is beyond the realm of science and technology. This ancient, anxious, and argued question finds its answer only in Christ. The Risen Lord alone could declare with ultimate authority: "He who believes in me will live, even though he dies" (John 11:25). The resurrection of Jesus Christ once and for all indisputably answered Job's age-old question, "If a man dies, will he live again?"

Beethoven's 6th symphony sounds the crash of the storm, followed by the first tremulous notes of new hope, broadening into a song of thanksgiving. That is something of what happened between Good Friday and Easter. And because of that, when storm and death strike, we have a hope that is an anchor for the soul.

Christ's resurrection solved the riddle of death. It means that the worst has been met and conquered, and no matter what, the last word will be victory.

YOU CAN BE CONFIDENT IN CHRIST THAT DEATH IS NOT THE END BUT THE BEGINNING IN ETERNITY.

God will lift us up
from being a victim
to being a victor
in life's struggles.

61

FROM PIT TO PINNACLE

I know that my Redeemer lives. (Job 19:25)

With this affirmation, Job rose from his pit of futility to his pinnacle of faith. This textual jewel shines all the brighter because of its night-enshrouded setting. Christians have appropriated Job's staunch affirmation when we listen to the stirring soprano strains of Handel's Messiah.

In climbing high mountains we reach a point known as the "timberline" where the forest stops and only dwarf trees grow sparsely. Trees at these heights produce the most exquisite grain and resonant wood. Despite the blasts and twists of the wind or the wrenching fury of the storms, these trees endure the stresses and strains. An extra flow of resin is produced in the trees that gives them the elegant grain and rare timbre and resonance. The strain of survival in a severe climate produces fibers for the finest musical instruments from which will come the melodies that will enrich thousands of listeners.

Our lives, exposed to stresses and strains from the storms of life, when surrendered to the creative work of their Creator, can be endowed with beautiful texture and harmony that will resonate to the lives of others.

Job's suffering led him to one of the loftiest affirmations in the Bible. For each of us, our trials and sorrows can become a means to a deeper trust, a more steadfast faith, and a closer relationship with God, who will lift us from pit to pinnacle, from depths to heights, and from being a victim to a victor in life's struggles.

IN FAITH, YOU CAN SPEAK THESE WORDS, "I KNOW MY REDEEMER LIVES." GOD'S STRENGTH ENABLES YOUR ENDURANCE THROUGH LIFE'S TRIALS.

Death is the last step of life that leads into the eternal presence of God.

PRECIOUS DEATH

Precious in the sight of the LORD
is the death of his saints. (Ps. 116:15)

To us on earth, the loss of a loved one in death is a heavy sorrow. But the Word of God tells us that to God, the death of one of His own is "precious."

When God created the world, He looked upon the work of His hands and pronounced it "good." But none of that handiwork was called "precious" in His sight. The death of the saints, however, is precious in His sight. The people of God are of far greater worth to Him than all the planets and stars of His creation. What a blessed assurance that we are that precious to God.

Why is the death of the believer singled out as precious to God? It is the moment in which the believer is received in the eternal embrace of his Heavenly Father. It is the moment in which the soul goes from the toil of the world to the rest God has prepared, from the labors of the earth to the rewards of eternity, from the sorrows of this world to the eternal joys of heaven, from the temporal fellowships of earth to eternal fellowship with God and the people of God.

Death, which many consider a terror, becomes a triumph for the child of God. For the saint, death is the coronation or the last step of life that leads into the eternal presence of God.

For those who know Christ, death becomes the most precious moment of life. In death, we shall see our Savior and Lord face to face and enter into the eternal joys of Heaven. And our home-coming to loved ones who have gone on before will also be precious in their sight!

YOU ARE PRECIOUS IN GOD'S EYES.

The Lord speaks again
his assuring promise,
"Peace be with you."

THE GIFT OF PEACE

Peace be with you. (John 20:19)

Suddenly, a presence stood in the midst of Jesus' disciples. The moment was electric with suspense. "Could this be ...? Has Jesus come back from the dead?"

In this moment, Jesus' spoken words were supremely important to them. Like soft music floating through the night air, in the stillness of the room among His transfixed followers His words are heard, "Peace be with you."

Peace? In the midst of the death and defeat at Calvary? Peace? In the midst of their great sorrow? Peace? When their fortunes were blackest? Peace? When all their hopes and dreams had been nailed to a humiliating cross at their "Ground Zero"?

But the risen Lord chose "peace" as the word to His followers. He spoke it twice to His grief-stricken disciples. "Peace," He said to them and shattered their gloom.

Who dared to speak this word to them? Jesus,

the one who conquered death, the "king of terrors." He burst forth from the tomb and turned history's great tragedy into its greatest triumph. And what is the word of the risen Lord to us today? What does the resurrected One say to our troubled and tortured world; a world haunted with fear, filled with strife, wars, turmoil, terrorism?

His gift of peace is still given to His followers today. Peace is not a matter of circumstances, nor even of security in our world of violence. It is a matter of the heart. The Lord comes to us in the midst of our failures, fears, sorrows, and tragedies and speaks again His assuring promise, "Peace be with you."

GOD'S PEACE CAN FILL YOUR LIFE DESPITE
ANY TRIAL OR CIRCUMSTANCE.

In the darkness
God opens to us
His richest treasures.

SCARS INTO STARS

I will give you the treasures of darkness,
riches stored in secret places. (Isa. 45:3)

"You can take away my wife, you can take away my children, you can strip me of my clothes and my freedom, but there is one thing no person can ever take away from me—and that is my freedom to choose how I will react to what happens to me." Dr. Viktor Frankl, author of the book, *Man's Search for Meaning,* spoke these words as he stood before the Gestapo. The Nazis in the Second World War stripped Frankl naked. His wife, children, and parents were all killed in the holocaust.

"Sweet are the uses of adversity" wrote William Shakespeare. History powerfully preaches that truth. Lock him in a prison cell, and you have a John Bunyan. Bury him in the snows of Valley Forge, and you have a George Washington. Raise him in horrible poverty, and you have an Abraham Lincoln. Deafen him, and you have a Beethoven.

Have him or her born black in a society filled with racism, and you have a Marian Anderson or a Martin Luther King. Call him a slow learner, and you have an Albert Einstein.

It's not what happens to us on the outside that matters; it's what is on the inside that counts. Faith in God can turn our scars into stars, our sorrows into servants, our obstacles into opportunities, our tragedies into triumphs, our stresses into strengths, and our stumbling blocks into stepping stones.

The Creator has precious gems and gold, oil and coal, and many other riches "stored in secret places." And as Isaiah reminds us, it is in the darkness of our lives that He opens to us His richest treasures.

> YOUR FAITH IN GOD CAN TURN
> YOUR TRAGEDY INTO TRIUMPH.

God's power turns life's cruel misfortunes into treasures.

NOT WHY, BUT WHO?

But now my eyes have seen you. (Job 42:5)

The Chinese word for crisis uses a combination of two characters, which designate 'danger' and 'opportunity.' This is true for every crisis. It is a turning point, and depending on which way a person turns, he can find danger or opportunity.

When an oyster gets an irritating grain of sand in its shell, it grows a pearl around it and turns an irritation into something of beauty. Like the oyster, in the power of God we can turn life's cruel misfortunes into treasures.

Sixteen times in his book Job hurled to the heavens his anguished cry, "Why?" But God never answered this question. Fifty-nine times we encounter the word Who in reference to God. The simple change of a *y* to an *o* made all the difference.

Job did not need to know why. He just needed to know who—who was in control, who cared for him, who would sustain and vindicate him. We do

70

not need so much an explanation of God as we do an experience with God. Job's healing came when his preoccupation with why gave way to a submission and trust in who.

Marlene Chase writes, "At the apex of suffering it seems that nothing helps, all that is left to do is to lie in the dust of our dead dreams. But then the warm breath of God comes upon us and we can hardly believe the subtle surprise upon waking that we are whole again."

Job came to a new and deeper awareness of God and experienced a wholeness he had not known before. When in the Lord's strength we arise from our "Ground Zero," the same breathtaking opportunity awaits us.

IN THE POWER OF GOD, YOU CAN TURN
LIFE'S MISFORTUNES INTO TREASURES.

Life must go on.

STRENGTH FOR THE DAYS AHEAD

In the previous pages, we have had numerous reflections on the insights and inspiration from the Word of God that speak to us in time of trouble. Complete healing of any time that life gets tough will not take place in a few days or a few weeks. Life must go on, and we need a strategy to be victors over and not victims of our experiences. The following suggestions provide additional steps of healing for the days ahead.

FIND GOD'S TREASURE IN THE DARKNESS

Earlier in this book, we reflected on the promise, "I will give you the treasures of darkness" (Isa. 45:3). When we turn our trouble over to God, He brings forth a treasure from it. What a loss it would be to suffer noncreatively and not to become a better person from our suffering. What a tragedy if you are diminished rather than enriched from what God has done in and for us. Your treasure may spring from a new and liberating insight or truth that will continue to enrich

72

your life. Or possibly you have bonded with a loved one or a friend in a deeper way. Or your experience has birthed a new sensitivity and perspective on life and its priorities. Or you have taken a giant step of spiritual and personal growth. Identify the treasure from God in your hour of darkness. Thank Him for it and go on to use it for His glory and your further healing.

Reach out to Someone Else

Use what you have learned from your experience to reach out and help lift another person's burden. In comforting us, God makes us comforters. The apostle Paul affirms, "The Father of compassion and the God of all comfort, who comforts us in all our troubles, so that we can comfort those in any trouble with the comfort we ourselves have received from God" (2 Cor. 1:3–4). A person who has suffered has the most to give to others. One of the best therapies in life comes from helping and encouraging someone else. This act of kindness to others lifts us out of ourselves and gives us encouragement from our comfort to others.

73

Live Daily with the Word of God

Adopt a reading and meditation plan for a daily time with the Bible. Other books are given for our information. The Bible is given for our transformation. There's a big difference between the books that men make and the Book that makes men. "Your word is a lamp to my feet and a light for my path" said the psalmist (119:105). The Bible is our guidebook, and it sheds knowledge on adversity—the best antidote for suffering people. God's Word will be a servant for our growth, a stepping-stone and resource for the journey, and a light for our unknown future.

Claim God's Special Promise

The Bible is filled with promises; in fact there are an astounding 8,810 of them. These promises of God cover the spectrum of human need. God gives to us a promise for every problem. When the storms of life hit with hurricane force, God has promised in His Word, "When you pass through the waters, I will be with you" (Isa. 43:2). The key word is through. He will bring us through our difficulties. No wave is too high, no crashing breaker is too strong, and no undertow is too formidable. As we trust in God's strength, we will not go down, but through. He has brought us through, and now He will lead us on. Search God's Word, find the special promise He has for you, write it down, memorize it, frame and display it, then go on and live by it.

Develop Your Prayer Life

"Out of the depths I cry to you, O LORD," is the plaintive cry of the psalmist (130:1). We, too, have called to God from the depths, from the deep pain, suffering, shock, and trouble that had come into our lives. Prayer is the secret weapon of the child of God. In prayer, our weakness is linked to Almightiness, our ignorance to Infinite Wisdom, and our future to Divine Guidance. Make prayer a priority on your schedule for a particular daily time and place. Include various types of prayer: adoration, confession, thanksgiving, petition, intercession, and submission.

MAKE FRIENDS WITH GREAT HYMNS

In the previous pages, we reflected on how God "gives songs in the night." Surround yourself with recordings of sacred music, listen to them often, and let their inspiration seep deep into your soul. Secure a church hymnbook, and let it be a companion to your Bible. It is a treasure trove of devotional poems of prayer and praise that can immeasurably enrich your life. Memorize the hymns that speak to you, sing them, alone if need be and even through tears, until their mighty truths bring their comfort and strength to your soul.

WALK FORWARD

You have a life to live. There are people who need you, and with whom you need to be involved. Be proactive. Join a support group if needed. Link up with a fellowship group, perhaps in a Bible study. When one problem has passed, it's time to get ready for the next one. Use these steps to strengthen foundations of life, and be prepared to face the next problem. There are no graduates in the school of pain. Sooner or later we will be further tested in our faith and the foundations of our life. Our Lord has promised strength to nourish our spirit, even if our physical suffering goes unrelieved. He Himself has hurt and bled and suffered. He comes beside us on our road of sorrow. He ministers to us through His Spirit and through members of His body who bear us up and relieve our suffering. He enables us to go forward to our relationships, our duties, opportunities, and challenges that are before us. Let us in faith pray daily, "Lord, help me to remember that nothing can happen today that You and I cannot handle together!"

Psalm 23

The LORD is my shepherd
I shall not be in want.
He makes me lie down in green pastures,
He leads me beside quiet waters, He restores my soul.
He guides me in the paths of righteousness
For his name's sake.
Even though I walk through the valley
Of the shadow of death,
I will fear no evil,
For you are with me;
Your rod and your staff,
They comfort me.
You prepare a table before me
In the presence of my enemies.
You anoint my head with oil;
My cup overflows.
Surely goodness and love will follow me
All the days of my life,
And I will dwell in the house of the LORD forever.

ABOUT THE AUTHOR

Colonel Henry Gariepy, B.A., M.S., author of over 20 books, served as National Editor in Chief for The Salvation Army until 1995. His works include biography, history, and devotional genres.

In addition, he has contributed chapters to 15 books, an essay in the Wesleyan NIV Reflecting God Study Bible, numerous articles in domestic and overseas periodicals, and devotional series for the radio program "Wonderful Words of Life."

In his 'active retirement' he teaches theology and church history as an adjunct faculty, serves as a Literary Consultant, and teaches at Bible Seminars and Writers' Conferences. At his home church he teaches the Adult

Bible Class and serves in a lay leadership position. He is an outdoor enthusiast, finished three 26-mile marathons, and with his wife, Marjorie, takes great joy in his four children and twelve grandchildren.